Dream Teaching

JUN – – 2014

Dream Teaching

Edwin Romond

Grayson Books

West Hartford, Connecticut

Grayson Books
P. O. Box 270549
W. Hartford, CT 06127

Printed in the United States of America

Library of Congress Cataloging-in-Publication Data

Romond, Edwin.
  Dream teaching / Edwin Romond.
      p. cm.
  ISBN 0-9675554-8-5
  1. English teachers—Poetry. 2. Education—Poetry. 3. Teaching—Poetry.
  4. Schools—Poetry. I. Title.
  PS3618.O655D74 2005
  811'.6—DC22

                        2004029101

Acknowledgements

Grateful acknowledgement is given to the editors of these publications, where some of the poems in this book first appeared.

A Fine Frenzy: Poets Respond to Shakespeare: Lady Macbeth, Afterward

Art of Music: Everything about Egypt

Black River Review: In Praise of Janitors

Ekphrasis: For Laura Wingfield

The English Journal: "At Night the Characters on My Shelves Come Out to Party," Copyright © by NCTE, 1993, "The Boy Who Stutters," Copyright © by NCTE, 2003, "Retirement," Copyright © by NCTE, 2004, Reprinted with permission. "Dream Teaching," Copyright © 1998 by Edwin Romond.

In Love United: A 9/11 Anthology: Picking Up My Son after His First Day of Pre-School, September 11, 2001

Karamu: Harold Crinkley, Faithful Husband, Calls Home from the Teachers' Convention

Lip Service: The Fullback and the Dancer

New Jersey Council of Teachers of English Journal: First Day – First Year, When I Heard the Learned Administrator

Poet Lore: Father Dismas, Gregorian Chant Teacher

Pudding: Seeing and Believing

Rockhurst Review: To the Girl Who Wasn't Asked to the Prom

The Sun: Letter to My Principal

The Teacher's Journal: Classroom Fight on Monday

Voices: The Journal of the American Academy of Psychotherapists: Morning after a Student Dies

Warren County Companion: Gentian in Autumn

for Mary and for Liam

Contents

Dream Teaching

I am first in line for coffee
and the copier is not broken yet.
This is how dreams begin in teaching high school.

First period the boy who usually carves skulls
into his desk raises his hand instead
to ask about *Macbeth* and, for the first time,
I see his eyes are blue as melting ice.
Then, those girls in the back
stop passing notes and start taking them
and I want to marvel at tiny miracles
but still another hand goes up
and Butch the drag racer says he found the meaning
in that Act III soliloquy. Then more hands join the air
that is now rich with wondering and they moan
at the bell that ends our class and I ask myself,
"How could I have thought of calling in sick today?"

I open my eyes for the next class and no one's late,
not even Ernie who owns his own time zone
and they've all done their homework
that they wave in the air
because everyone wants to go to the board
to underline nouns and each time I turn around
they're looking at me as if I know something
they want and, steady as sunrise, they do everything right.

At lunch the grouchy food lady discovers smiling
and sneaks me an extra meatball. In the teachers' room
we eat like family and for twenty-two minutes
not one of us bitches about anything.
Then the afternoon continues the happiness of hands

wiggling with answers and I feel such a spark
when spike-haired Cindy in the satanic tee shirt
picks the right pronoun and glows like a saint.

And me, I'm up and down the room now, cheering,
cajoling, heating them up like a revival crowd.
I'm living only in exclamatory sentences. They want it all
and I'm thinking, "What drug are we on here?"
Just as Crusher Granorski screams, "Predicate nominatives
are awesome!" the principal walks in
with my check and I say, "That's okay,
you can keep it." When the bell sounds
they stand, raise lighted matches
and chant, "Adverbs! Adverbs!"
I drive home petting my plan book.

At night I check the weather without wishing for a blizzard,
then sleep in the sweet maze of dreams
where I see every student from 32 years of school days:
boys and girls, sons and daughters who're almost mine,
thousands of them stretching like dominoes into the night
and I call the roll and they sing, "We're all here, Mr. Romond!"
When I pick up my chalk they open their books,
look up and, with eager eyes, ask me to teach them.

Seeing and Believing

The girls giggled
but the boys laughed right out loud
when Mrs. Stone raged crimson
holding my eighth grade project:
"The Map of New Jersey."

"Get up here, boy!"
and I had no choice
but to walk the gangplank to her desk
where my map choked in her fist.

"What's this jazz? Huh?
The ocean is not green, Bub, it's blue.
Ya' get it? Blue, blue, blue, blue!"
punching my map with each word into my chest.
My classmates roared a chorus
of "Green ocean! Green ocean!"
their voices rising in waves of laughter

as I carried the wrinkled and ripped map
back to my seat through their sneers.
Soon, all their maps perimetered the room,
leaving me adrift in the memory of a Sunday

when, in the October air,
my father and I walked over seashells
and I, only nine,
remarked that the ocean looked green.
My father, peering out from beneath his cap,
said, "Yes, it does" and his fingers swam
through my hair.

Everything about Egypt
for Sister Judith

Music was only supposed to last
from 12:20 to one but
on St. Patrick's Day Sister Judith
seemed radiant as star dust
so on we sang
holding the geography of Egypt
for another day. I remember
our forty-two faces lighting
with Sister's love for the songs
of Ireland that afternoon. Egyptian
rivers had to wait while Vito
Carluzzi crooned, "When Irish
Eyes Are Smiling" and Stash
Jankowski belted "Me Father's
Shillelagh." We just kept singing
and singing with the pyramids and
sphinxes growing one day older
for soon it was 1:30, then it was two
in a room filled with fifth graders
and a nun we loved, one
voice beautiful as prayer. And I,
like a lucky leprechaun, found
a pot of gold in the second row
where pretty Jane Ellen Hughes
sang "O Danny Boy" and I dreamed
in green she was really singing
"O Eddie Boy" as we walked hand
in hand along a Galway shore.
So, Sister Judith, lovely lady of God,
know that this boy in the back
remembers when we kept text books

closed to spend all afternoon in song
and that joy is an emerald river
flowing through my soul and all these years
later I need to thank you for everything
about Egypt we did not learn the day
you let the lesson plan go, one March 17th
when none of us could stop the music.

Father Dismas, Gregorian Chant Teacher

That day I belched from the back
and got the whole class snorting as he sat
at the upright pressing sober notes
of *Missa XXIII*, I would not confess
when he shouted, "Who did that? Who?"
I just crouched behind Falkowski.
The class winced till he said,
"Everyone get out," but no one moved.
Not one stood to leave the class
that was a joke last period, Mondays,
with the 80 year old priest.

"Get out!" he said again, then turned his back
as we shoved our *Liber Usalis* into our book bags.
In the hall, under the plaster eyes of Jesus,
no one would look at me.
But, when they shunned me outside
I trudged back into school, resigned
to appease him for my friends.

I coughed in the doorway
but he played on, his eyes shut
and again I coughed,
but he only played louder,
his silver hair shaking
as he murmured the Latin.
All I could do was stand there
as he played to the empty chairs.
I had come back to clean the slate
with an easy detention but he ignored me
and played till the chapel bell chimed 4 o'clock.
Then he placed his hands on his knees.

"Father, I did it, but I didn't mean to."
He just stared at the keyboard.
"This is God's music, Edwin,"
he said softly. Then he struggled to his feet
and left the room,
taking home his stacks of song sheets
like gifts at a party
that no one would open.

First Day - First Year

Jerstad-Agerholm Junior High School
Racine, Wisconsin, 1971

I wore lime green bell bottoms and confidence
as convincing as I could fake when the first
period class walked in. Matt Adams, Tim Brown,
Jill Boske, Lisa Cain, they all became lives
in my seating chart, six rows of 14 year olds,
hormones brewing, self-conscious, silent until

I misread Arnold Rutlicker as *Arnold Butt-licker*,
after which everyone relaxed except Arnold.
I previewed the great stuff we'd learn
like semi-colons, active voice, and indicative mood.
I psyched them up for first novel: the spine-
tingling *Johnny Tremain*. I promised thrills

of filmstrips titled: "Here Come the Conjunctions!"
"Don't Dangle That Participle!" and "Have Fun
with Footnotes!" Then nervous Ned Nukowski,
who valued the nutrition of breakfast, threw up
Fruit Loops on Laurie Kent's Partridge Family
book bag. I had four classes to go.

Name after name became face after face, a parade
of Jennifers and Jims, Karens and Toms, Tammys,
Kevins, one guy named Angus, and Bertha
who asked to be called Trixie. My eighth graders
in stiff new blue jeans took their seats to become
members of my life this September 3rd, my first day

as Mr. Romond, English teacher. Who knows what
they thought as my hotcombed hair swelled
like an aroused Brillo pad and sweat turned
my shirt into a polyester sponge. Still,
many drew smiles on their papers
and Arnold yelled, "See you tomorrow, Mr. Bone!"

when I sat in my '66 Pontiac where I peeled open
my collar, leaned back, and closed my eyes.
I thought of my students' essays in my new brief case,
their young handwriting unlocking their lives. On WOKY
Chicago belted, *Only the beginning, only just the start.*
I turned it up, stepped on the gas, and sang my way home.

The Boy Who Stutters

He's been silent since the first day
when he stammered asking to sit
in the last seat back by the cabinet.
Now, a week later, I call on him
to speak about last night's assignment,
the one about tragic flaws. He stares
at me as if I have betrayed him
and taps his feet when twenty-eight heads
turn to hear him *Sha-Sha-Sha*
into *Shakespeare*. I fight the urge
to finish his words for him,
to speed my class along and
save all of us the discomfort
of his fractured speech sounding
like prayers of a dying bird.
Here, where each class is planned
for three weeks in advance
and my grade book is ledger-perfect,
he struggles, red-faced, forcing me
to learn about learning. So I stop
myself and let him stagger
through his ideas about Hamlet,
Macbeth, and Lear. When he's done,
there's nothing for me to do but love
his eyes as he watches the class
open their notebooks
to save everything they've learned
from his trembling lips.

Teaching My Father

I'd tell him to write what he knows,
be specific about trucks and warehouses,
the best roads from Newark to Perth Amboy.
I'd teach him to turn abstract into concrete,
turn *love* into those Almond Joys
he'd bring my mother, turn *trust* into keys
store owners gave him to their doors.
If he hesitated about his handwriting,
if he worried about how it would look,
I'd tell him to print it, just let it out,
there's nothing he could put on paper
I wouldn't love. He could check that black
pocket dictionary he kept in his work shirt
and, in my classroom, he could even
wear his speckled cap as he wrote the essay,
What I Never Had the Chance to Tell You.
And, if writer's block is a problem, I'd say,
"Let me help you open your life into language.
Dear Father, bless me with your wisdom
and I'll share with you my learning.
I am your son, there's so much now
we could teach each other."

The Fullback and the Dancer

Joy had been a headlock or towel sting
in the damp blur of the showers
where he could hide in the vulgar

alphabet of boys hardening into men,
who'd mastered the harshness
of males who only bare their bodies.

But then she was beautiful there, alone
on the talent show stage,
her muscular legs slashing the air

as his friends laughed and hooted
around him. But he heard only
the strange music and knew it was wings

for her feet that launched her again
and again into a sky of blue light
that bathed her curves and made him crave

her softer strength she held like crystal.
And so utterly lonely she made him
among his teammates belching in the back.

So he left to take the back way home,
alone, using silence to play her music,
to see her move and feel again

the pain of her pleasure throbbing
like the sweet ache of freezing feet
near a stove. Suddenly,

he tried to hoist all of himself
into a shaking pirouette,
his shadow trembling like a new-born

as he dreamed he was lifting her high
into the street lamp spotlight,
his muscles rippling with the weight of grace,

his tough blood dancing from his heart.

Gentian in Autumn

All through school they were falling in love,
the halls were a tangle of arms each morning
as students stoked the fires of desire and touch.
But this teacher stared it all away

and traveled his days feeling nothing
like love or longing, pains he'd sworn off
for the safety of distance,
that cold anesthesia for the wounded.

Even a cynic could turn to the Divine
to show how joy can rise from need,
emerging like a life
of shoreline to sailors who had given up.

But he knows it was the shock of Christmas
in September that made him stop and look
where the pretty new music teacher
waved 50 voices into beauty, her hands

luring them from the growl
of rock and roll to the sounds of peace on earth.
In him she stirred an urge as she moved
to the rhythm pulsing from the rows of singers.

So he set down his books and whispered along,
like a man learning to speak again.
Then he saw her hair glossing like chestnuts
and he pictured his apartment and supper alone,

and wondered if he were young enough to hope
she might smile should he walk in
to introduce himself, his nervous heart
a gentian in autumn, blooming to her music.

Snow Day

It's sleigh bells,
that phone ringing at 6 a.m.
and the mumble of a sleepy voice
about snow and canceled school.
I rise like a death row convict
who's just been called by the governor
and give out in the darkness a scream
that would make Tarzan need throat spray
as I proceed to dance the "Funky Chicken"
in my pajamas, hopping like Michael Jackson
if he were electrocuted. Then I dive
back into bed, deep into the warm
tunnels of blankets where I dream
of teaching Miss January
the troublesome verbs of "lie" and "lay"
as outside the snow white-chalks
the wind, erasing everything
I had to do today.

At Night the Characters on My Classroom Shelves Come Out to Party

Capt. Ahab peers in his telescope and yells, "All clear!"
and the rest unpage from the bindings of shelf life.
Gatsby's first in his golden Rolls, screeching around,
nearly hitting Laura Wingfield, who's with Stanley Kowalski,
her latest hope from the Literary Computer Dating Service.
And there's Macbeth lecherously proclaiming, "Tonight
and tonight and tonight!" as he watusis with the witches,
which irritates Jonathan Edwards who's mingling
and telling everyone to go to hell. The Duke and the King
try to sell Mississippi time shares to Hester, but she's busy
with my grade book changing all the marks to "A's."
And there's Old Rip scribbling on my desks, "This class
puts me to sleep," but Blanche DuBois is really in trouble
depending on the kindness of strange Edgar Allan Poe
who's moaning how lovely she'd look in a casket.
Then "Better Late Than Never" Reverend Dimmesdale
preaches from *Planned Parenthood Journal* to Oscar Wilde,
who is not interested. The party's getting hot now
which makes Lady Macbeth tell the fur-coated Jack London,
"Off, off, dammed coat!" just as the cast of "The Lottery"
arrives to suggest that everyone get stoned. They all go wild
till poet Emily, who never left the shelf to begin with,
peeks out to whisper, "Homeroom!" and they all scurry back
like illegal aliens. But poor Hamlet can't find *Hamlet*
so he jumps into "The Lady or the Tiger?" where he stares
at both doors before turning to the crowd to warn,
"You'd better get comfortable. This might take a while."

Lady Macbeth, Afterward

Was it the ghoul in you that craved sex
after murder, that desired a husband
trembling with another man's blood?
Or was it the corpse of a king,
a hallway away, daggered in his last dream,
that became your aphrodisiac? Outside,
owls stabbed at falcons and stallions
gnawed each other but in bed it was your hands
that had their way, pulling his face
to your breasts, leading him into you,
you, who bragged you had unsexed yourself,
even you became inflamed with what the living
live for. And afterward, when you recited,
"I love you," he answered with crazed silence
as lightning flashed your windows
like eyes of a furious God.

Pregnant Student

Big
so terribly
big
sticking out
like a beach ball
in a playpen
she can barely
squeeze her belly
behind the desk
and no one stares
anymore
and she meets
the eyes of no one
just gives
to her journal
her life
and another
where she tells me
she dreamed
last night
of two birds
in cages
the shameless eyes
of those waiting
to fly.

Morning after a Student Dies

My class sits silently long beyond "a moment
of silence" from the P.A. Some weep, most stare
into the quiet for grief has left us only breath
of the heater and the rustle of legs under desks.

When they do speak, it's *Not fair!* over
and over, furious, terrified by cancer at sixteen
and I envy their faith that life's a promise
of goodness, a creed I gave up long ago.

Still, I yearn to be wise, to stun their pain.
But I'm lost in my own darkness. Michael's seat,
solemn as a shrine in the third row, is one more
reminder that the best of love leaves us behind.

I almost utter something like, *Seize life!*
Love while you can! but Becky and Sue grieve
in a trembling embrace and part of me longs
to go to them, press what's left of my heart

to their hearts and, right in front of everyone,
be a living man. I choose instead the safety
of attendance and tally who's here, who's not;
by black lead checks, the scratching of the dead.

Letter to My Principal

I came to school late today
and I am sorry.
I do remember your note
about my punctuality
but a calf was born last night
and I found him blinking
into his first morning
and, Sir,
he was so tiny and white,
like a dab of marshmallow
upon the spearmint grass.
So, please understand
I was caught in a sunrise
so gold it turned our barn
to pink and sponged the dew
where the calf lay startled
at the light after life
in the black pond of the womb.
I was set to leave, I swear I was,
but his mother, her eyes dark plums,
began to bathe him with her tongue
moving like a paint brush
up and down his milky face.
And when he gazed at me
and mooed like a nervous bassoon,
what could I do but stay
until he stood on his own
and began to tiptoe
as if the grass were eggs?

Classroom Fight on Monday

The one who's absent might whine
that she missed this. The rest form a circle,
as if ritual, around the hot-faced
quarterback and tackle, best friends screaming
about some Jennifer and Saturday night.
Then fists flail like snapped wires ignited
by an energy alien to my class of Wordsworth
and Whitman. The back of my room
never seemed so far as I stumble through desks
spilled like stools in a barroom brawl
and, through cheering students, watch blood
from Mike's face dot the floor
as Ken keeps him in a headlock and pummels
his knee up into Mike's chest.
They shout language with all their might
till Mike shoves free and sends Ken skull first
into the cinder block wall and I can't reason
any longer with my students blocking me
like linemen. So I put my hands on Cindy
who'd held the door for me this morning
and shove her too hard and she looks at me
with so much hurt I almost stop before
bear-hugging Ken and shouting, "Stop!
Please, stop!" But he knifes his elbow back
into my stomach that hasn't felt a punch
in thirty years and that second I want
to hurt him in front of his yelping classmates
whose eyes blaze with a dark glee
that turns them into strangers.
And I hate them all
acting like the dead when I plead for help
as Ken and Mike keep fighting

with me holding on.
After hall guards rush in
and drag them off like wrecked race cars
I walk up to my desk wiping blood
from my tie, then turn to face my students.
Some search for their breath; others
text message friends, their urgent fingers
telling what they loved about my class today.

Harold Crinkley, English Teacher, Gets Revenge in the Boys' Lav

He had had it
with monitoring that stench
of smoke and urine and those punks
who elbowed past him cackling,
"Chill out, Dude!" and then
those scoundrels who mumbled,
"Crinkley's a geek!"

But when he beheld his named smeared
on the stalls with misspelled perversions
and blotched across walls like a rash,
he glared through his bifocals and swore

he would skip the library Friday night
to stalk the yearbook like a sheriff
and round up the names he needed.
All night he sat with pen and paper,
chugging hot milk, grimly setting about
the revenge any real man would demand.
In his sleep he was grizzly Clint Eastwood
hanging them high from handles of giant urinals.

Next day he started his station wagon,
shut his eyes and murmured, "Do what you've got to do."

The weekend custodian vaguely recalled a man
in Bermudas and wing tips swaggering
through school with fists of Magic Markers.

On Monday the lav was a tangle of boys
straining to read the stencil-perfect script:

> *Slobnewski has the vocab of a cinder block*
> *and Grimsley thinks Edgar Allan Poe is a law firm.*
> *When Staley has a brain storm it's a passing shower.*
> *If Bailey's face were a word, it'd be misspelled.*
> *If Wilson's nose were a sentence, it'd be a run-on,*
> *and if Snyder had been Huck Finn, Jim would've drowned him.*

All day Crinkley wore a sinister grin
as he strutted the halls with his book bag.
But when the last bell emptied the school,
he locked himself in the lav
to savor the lines of his handiwork.
He leaned against a sink
and drew markers from his pants like six guns.
If he had to, he would strike again.

At the English Teachers' Insane Asylum

You must be crazy to teach here.
Mrs. Hadley, who loved too much
the smiles of students, dances the halls
grinning into wall tiles. Mr. Tackwitz
thinks he's a "Works Cited" page and
greets friends alphabetically by last name
including Simpson and Dexter.
One swears he's a period, the other
a comma. Between shock treatments
they're a walking semi-colon.

Mr. Crane, whose principal wrote him up
for uneven shades, keeps his clothes
in a seating chart and gives assignments
to grapes in his Fruit of the Looms
that he grades while listening to tapes
of favorite phone calls from parents.
Next door, a private academy teacher
suffers from visions of SAT scores
in his toilet. Night after night the poor man
flushes and flushes, screaming analogies.

This is the home of tweed straight jackets and those
who can't believe it's Sunday without essays to grade.
At night they speak in their sleep. Some recite
the complimentary notes they never received
and cry, "Thank you, thank you!" into their pillows.
Mr. Steck thinks tomorrow's the first day of school
and wakes sweating again and again and in Room 666
Mrs. Vail screams as she dreams of a class
with Jack the Ripper and Dracula. She hears the moon
remind her it's a teacher's job to reach them.

To the Girl Who Wasn't Asked to the Prom

You were the only one in my class to feel
for Amanda Wingfield and let her ache
wound your heart. Your essay was a dirge
for her loneliness and I learned you knew
what it meant to be abandoned and need
what you don't have. On this May Friday,
spring's dressed up for love but you sit
among the empty desks of those dismissed
early for prom hair cuts and tux rentals.
And, while you read next week's homework,
I wish, for just tonight, I could be seventeen
and handsome, some fantasy prince to give
you something to talk about on Monday
when the halls will be loud with stories.
As long as I'm making fiction,
I could sketch us waltzing until midnight
and then a long, slow drive to the shore
where we'd find what moved Byron
and Keats to poetry. I take necessary safety
in knowing you will never see what I write
to you here behind my briefcase for I do love
my wife and I'd hate to see myself
in the newspaper with other middle-aged men
and "name-withheld" minors. I write this
only because your blue eyes are swelling
behind Chopin's *The Awakening* and I fear
you think romance will never touch your life,
that the rose of your heart is not good enough
to be picked. Perhaps tonight you would change
your mind if only I could ask you to dance.

One Wrestler

Sometimes I find him walking the halls, skipping lunch.
After Thanksgiving he begins to shrink in his clothes
and talks about "making weight." He is the only one

to refuse a cupcake at our class party. His eyes
twitch on days of matches, sometimes he fears
the scale so much he spits into the cup he hides

behind *For Whom the Bell Tolls.* I worry about this boy
who starves himself to win or lose before hundreds,
who must get close as a lover to battle some stranger.

And I ache when he gets locked into a cradle till the ref
slaps the mat and, as he walks off, I know he knows
those cheers are for another, each groan is for only him.

Parent Conference

She's here because I'm out of sync
with her son, Simon, whom I upset
with an F on his essay,
"A Comparison of Shakespeare
to the Rock Group, *Orgasmic Armpit.*"
She doesn't know how much more
she can take so she unfolds
a reprint from *The National Enquirer*,
"When Your Son Is a Genius,"
and quotes what I must do
to make him feel "number 1!"
When I won't wear a tee shirt
emblazoned, "I Am Simon's Teacher
but He's Really Teaching Me,"
she opens a letter to the school board
written by her attorney. I report
that her son spends class time
licking the print from his text book
and she reads a note from his therapist
stating, "Simon generates non-productive
energy if confronted about his disinclination
to commence cognitive tasks" then one
from his scout master that says, "if Simon is asked
to pitch a tent, he urinates on the campfire."
I offer the solution that Simon do
his assignments but she warns me
of the mailman on *America's Most Wanted*
who was forced to read a poem and,
38 years later, wiped out a post office
with a machine gun screaming,
"The woods are lovely, dark and deep
but I have promises to keep!"

"I hope you've learned something!" she says,
and grants me one last chance to shape up.
She'll be back at mid-quarter
to report on my progress.

My Wife Plants Petunias

It's the first day of summer
after a year at school
she would forget
if she could. In her eyes,
relief, as she kneels
among the bags of fertilizer
and top soil, comfortable
tangibles after classes
of sour faces, surly words

and her draining loneliness
at the front of the room.
I saw the dread in her face
as she buttoned her coat
each morning. I watched her
come home wounded, wanting
only to sit with tea and stare
out at the snow in our garden.
Around February I stopped asking,

"How was school?" knowing
the answer waited in the silence
at supper. This morning
I'd like to tell her how lovely
her hands look in canvas.
I consider pulling a flower
for her hair or maybe chasing
her with the hose but I see
she loves holding that petunia

like an infant's head before
tucking it into the opened earth.
So much hope teachers and
planters have that something
they do will seed to beauty.
I pain for my wife as she bends
to her flowers, watering,
nourishing, trying to believe
she can teach them to blossom.

For Laura Wingfield in
The Glass Menagerie

What can old phonograph records give you now
except someone else's scratched-up love to yearn for,
if you still have heart enough? But I wouldn't blame you
for giving up on the iron world beyond the apartment

smothered with your mother's boasts of jonquils
and gentleman callers. Laura, dear, these are hard times
for tenderness, and wishes on a fire escape
can't cure the cruelty of dancing with the one you love

when he loves another. Better to hold on to your glass
friends who glow in the affection of your hands and,
when songs from Paradise Dance Hall flow through rain,
don't blow out your candles. Next time, trust no one

who brags how big his shadow is.

In Praise of Janitors

I admit an envy for the work
of men who jiggle polishers past my door,
for the clean certainty of their labor,
how always they may look behind them
for the gleaming proof their work is not in vain.

In spring they purr mowers beyond my windows,
their faces glistening, while I dissolve in a suit
and tie, teaching the preference of action verbs.
And I praise old Arnie who rises above my class
to replace a bulb, who jokes from on high,

"Let there be light!" and there is.

To My Female Student Who Left a Note Stating, "I Hope Your Baby's Born Dead."

What was it, a lav pass
I wouldn't give you?
A quiz grade I wouldn't change?
Had I made you stop chewing gum?
Where does a teenage girl,
who is blessed with a womb
and the chance for children,
find the emptiness inside her
to write a death wish for a baby?

But, my anonymous student,
you didn't hate hard enough,
for my son's eyes light with a life
more beautiful than yours
will ever be and his tiny fingers
touch my lips with a softness
your heart could never hold.
See his red hair, bright as joy.

Listen to his voice cooing love from his crib.
And, when I kiss him, watch my face
almost erase the ache you caused me.
You, courageous scholar,
who waited until I was out sick
to leave your curse in ball point black,
look at Liam, our living son.
Just don't ask to hold him.

Picking Up My Son after His First Day of Pre-School
September 11, 2001

Last night he asked us over and over
if we had packed everything he'd need
for his first day of pre-school, his first time
away from us with people he didn't know.
And later, while he slept on sheets filled
with smiling Barneys, I lay in the next room
worrying about bullies and other terrors
that might be waiting within the walls
of Miss Rose's Sunshine Pre-School.

But when I arrive to pick him up
he wears the grin of a survivor and runs
across the room to tell me he's learned
a sunflower dance. "You have to open up
your arms," he says, "and pretend
you're reaching for the sky" and his eyes
are tiny suns as he waves his hands as high
as he can. It's then I clutch him to my heart,
grateful for his milk and cookie breath and

the beautiful ordinariness of one more day
of his life. And I don't want to let go,
I don't want to lead him out to my car
and the agony on the radio, the sagging
flags coloring our way home. I want to hide
him from today's sky where planes aimed
at death and changed his world with blood
and flames while he danced as a flower,
palms open, like a man gasping his last prayer.

With Our Six-Year-Old Son at the Lorraine Motel, Memphis, Tennessee

Since the time he learned to turn sound
into words Liam has asked us question
after question. Where does the sun sleep
at night? How does salt get into the sea?
Why is he the only one in his class with red hair?
But this boy with a Derek Jeter poster
above his bed, this boy who loves Bill Cosby
reruns, this boy whose Donavan McNabb
jersey is his second skin from September
to the Super Bowl, has never once asked
why people are different colors. This morning
at the Lorraine Motel he tells us his teacher
said Dr. King wanted everyone to be friends,
easier to grasp than bus boycotts, racial
integration, or Civil Rights legislation.
Liam knows only that King was a good man
and my wife and I are silent
when he asks why a good man is murdered.
We stand outside room 306, a wreath of
flowers on the spot where he fell. The guide
points across Mulberry St. to the window
where the gun was aimed and fired.
I will have to answer, "one bullet,"
should my son ask what does it take
in this world, to end a man with a dream?

When I Heard the Learned Administrator
after Walt Whitman

When I heard the learned administrator speak
in his omniscient in-service day voice to rows
of teachers, I recalled that he himself had not
taught a class in 30 years. And, as he covered
the screen with power point test score
numbers and chided us about ours being lower
than the next town's, he said this would be
in the papers and he dreaded the phone calls
from parents. After he ordered more work sheets,
drills, and test prep lessons aimed at the SAT
and ACT, this Ph.D. said the governor wanted
new state tests and what was he supposed to do
if that next town scored higher than we did?
When he, with a face red as his new Mercedes,
shouted about teachers' salaries being so high
with these numbers so low, when he asked
why in God's name were we teaching
if not to raise standardized tests scores,
I walked out past the coffee and doughnuts
into the perfect silence of the English wing.
I stood yearning for my unstatistical joy
when a weeping mother called to tell me
in her son's room next to Ozzie Osbourne
CD's, tins of chewing tobacco, and
under a *Guns and Ammo* magazine,
she found a poem he'd written in my class
titled, "Someone I Love" and
he had dedicated it to her.

Harold Crinkley, Faithful Husband, Calls His Wife from the Teachers' Convention

She never actually asked
but I want you to know
I would have said, "No,"
if she had. She didn't,
but I thought about her
suggesting and I confess
it was pleasant to consider
for she was beautiful and
I had had one more beer than two
and you know what happens
when that happens. But, it's okay,
no need to worry. We didn't do it
but I thought about it and was ready
to say, "No," but, as I just told you,
she didn't ask, although I did hope
she was interested but not too much
because it would have been hard
to keep my "No" up in the dark
since I missed you so much.
So, if I had said, "Yes," it would have been
only because she wore the same perfume
I bought you for our anniversary.
But, it's all right, I remained adamant
even though she never put into words
what I was thinking although I wished
she would but only so I could refuse her
for your sake.

Willy Loman

After I hit 50
I stayed
in the back
of my room
during *Death
of a Salesman.*
Some mornings
it was too much
to see
what comes
with the territory
of dreams
ringing up a zero
and I could not
let my class
catch their teacher
in tears
as you drove
your life
to a dead end
while I clutched
the script
like a mirror.

Science and English

for John Cosgrove

Sometimes you're asked to measure
the untouchable such as light
and sound. It all seems light years
away from the mysteries of poetry
but, like good friends, important
conversations, and nourishing
sharing, the beauty is in embracing
the questions, the joy grows
from knowing you will never reach
the ends of wonder. Physicists
and poets are brothers in a world
of questions and, like a good game
of baseball, it's not the ninth inning
that is the pleasure but the pitches
and swings that get you there.
This poem says thanks for the hall
that connects the Science and English
wings, thanks for the friendship
that grew over teachers' room coffee
and thanks for the love of everything
you and I still have to learn.

A Retiring Teacher Says Good-bye to Jim in Huckleberry Finn

At first my classes complained
they couldn't understand you,
your speech was foreign
language to their educated eyes.
But, as chapters peeled away,
the gold of your soul emerged
like moonlight in fog and words
like *loyalty* and *goodness*
appeared in my room and, Jim,
they were speaking about you.
Each school year I loved you
more and some nights I'd lie
awake wishing I could dive
into the pages and join you
and Huck on the raft floating
like a magnolia on the Mississippi,
away from the trash of hatred
on shore that makes us slaves
to ourselves. You soared above
dukes and kings and, by the end
of Chapter 43, we learned
who Huck's real father was, learned
how love shines through any syntax
and warms the deep waters
of our hearts. Long after I leave
Room 115 I'll still see you
steering through Missouri nights,
letting Huck sleep, standing tall
and noble, the brightest star
in the river's mirror of sky.

Retirement

The class didn't sing to me
as they did in *To Sir with Love*
and in this real world of Room 115
no Dead Poet stood on his desk
to call me, "Captain, my captain."
So I sit with the silence my last
students left behind and, if my life
were a film, there'd be music now,
haunted with minor chords, and,
instead of June's insistent sun,
rain would blur my windows.
Then desks would fill with ghosts
of students from 32 years, some
to thank me, others to remind me
I was not the one they needed.
So it ends as it was, an affair
with a demon lover, exhilarating
and heartbreaking, affirming
and ego crushing, muddled
as Christmas in middle age when
joy and grief wrestle in your heart.
I carry my vacant brief case out
past black boards waiting
for a younger person's writing.
Like book marks in a story
to be continued, I leave behind
my hunger for a different life,
my longing to do it all again.

To Future English Teachers
for BJ Ward

On those days
when you doubt where your heart has led you,
when classes seem an eternal lunch duty,
and driving home you feel like Willy Loman
lost between Brooklyn and Boston,
may you be able to recall for your soul's sake
at least one student. The one with live eyes
who'd stay after class to ask one more
question, whose face among rows of faces
hinted your lesson of the day might seed his life
of learning, one who met Whitman's verse
and began to make poems of his own.
May this student, like a good song,
visit you again and again, may you be blessed
with seeing him grow older and join hands
with you in adulthood. May you be dazzled
by what he now teaches you over beer
and a burger. And may you be wise enough
to learn what he's learned on his own, save it,
like a gift from a son, for all your future
students waiting in the years.

Order More Copies

To obtain copies of this book, send a check for $12.00 for each book, plus a $2.50 shipping & handling fee for your order to:

Grayson Books
P.O. Box 270549
West Hartford, CT 06107

Include your name, address, the number of copies you are ordering, and be sure to specify DREAM TEACHING as the book you are ordering.